THE WEAPONS ENCYCLOPÆDIA
TANK AIRCRAFT AFV SHIP ARTILLERY VEHICLES SECRET WEAPON

AF113269

TWE-034 ENG

✠ PANZER IV Sd.Kfz. 161

THE WEAPONS ENCYCLOPAEDIA

EDITORIAL STAFF
Luca Cristini, Paolo Crippa.

ACADEMIC STAFF
Enrico Acerbi, Massimiliano Afiero, Aldo Antonicelli, Ruggero Calò, Luigi Carretta, Flavio Chistè, Anna Cristini, Carlo Cucut, Salvo Fagone, Enrico Finazzer, Arturo Giusti, Björn Huber, Andrea Lombardi, Aymeric Lopez, Marco Lucchetti, Gabriele Malavoglia, Luigi Manes, Giovanni Maressi, Francesco Mattesini, Daniele Notaro, Péter Mujzer, Federico Peirani, Alberto Peruffo, Maurizio Raggi, Andrea Alberto Tallillo, Antonio Tallillo, Roberto Vela, Massimo Zorza.

PUBLISHED BY
Luca Cristini Editore (Soldiershop), via Orio, 35/4 - 24050 Zanica (BG) ITALY.

DISTRIBUTION BY
Soldiershop - www.soldiershop.com, Amazon, Ingram Spark, Berliner Zinnfigurem (D), LaFeltrinelli, Mondadori, Libera Editorial (Spain), Google book (eBook), Kobo, (eBoook), Apple Book (eBook).

PUBLISHING'S NOTES
None of unpublished images or text of our book may be reproduced in any format without the expressed written permission of Luca Cristini Editore (already Soldiershop.com) when not indicate as marked with license creative commons 3.0 or 4.0. Luca Cristini Editore has made every reasonable effort to locate, contact and acknowledge rights holders and to correctly apply terms and conditions to Content. Every effort has been made to trace the copyright of all the photographs. If there are unintentional omissions, please contact the publisher in writing at: info@soldiershop.com, who will correct all subsequent editions.

LICENSES COMMONS
This book may utilize part of material marked with license creative commons 3.0 or 4.0 (CC BY 4.0), (CC BY-ND 4.0), (CC BY-SA 4.0) or (CC0 1.0). We give appropriate attribution credit and indicate if change were made in the acknowledgments field. Our WTW books series utilize only fonts licensed under the SIL Open Font License or other free use license.

CONTRIBUTORS OF THIS VOLUME & ACKNOWLEDGEMENTS
We would like to thank the main contributors to this issue: The profiles of the tanks are all by the author. The colouring of the photos is by Anna Cristini. Special thanks to national and/or private institutions such as: Stato Maggiore dell'esercito, Archivio di Stato, Bundesarchiv, Nara, Library of Congress, Wikipedia, USAF, Signal magazine, Cronache di guerra, Fronte di guerra, IWM, Australian War Museum, ecc. A P.Crippa, A.Lopez, Péter Mujzer, L.Manes, C.Cucut, archivi Tallillo. Model Victoria (www.modelvictoria.it) ecc. for making available images or other items from their archives.

For a complete list of Soldiershop titles, or for every information please contact us on our website: www.soldiershop.com or www.cristinieditore.com. E-mail: info@soldiershop.com. Keep up to date on Facebook https://www.facebook.com/soldiershop.publishing

Title: **PANZER IV SD.KFZ. 161** Code.: **TWE-034 EN**
Series by: Luca Stefano Cristini
ISBN code: 9791255891949 first edition February 2025
THE WEAPONS ENCYCLOPAEDIA (SOLDIERSHOP) is a trademark of Luca Cristini Editore

THE WEAPONS ENCYCLOPÆDIA
TANK AIRCRAFT AFV SHIP ARTILLERY VEHICLES SECRET WEAPON

PANZER IV
SD.KFZ. 161

LUCA STEFANO CRISTINI

BOOK SERIES FOR MODELERS & COLLECTORS

CONTENTS

Introduction 5
  - Development 5
  - Technical characteristics 6

Versions of the vehicle 15
  - Panzer III Ausf. A - B - C -D 15
  - Panzer III Ausf. E - F 16
  - Panzer III Ausf. G - H - J - L - M - N 18
  - Other variants 20

Operational use 23

Camouflage and markings 41

Production and export 47

Data sheet 52

Bibliography 58

▲ Panzer IV Ausf. D. In addition to armour upgrades, the arc gun was reintroduced. Australian Armour and Artillery Museum.

INTRODUZIONE

The Panzerkampfwagen IV, commonly known as the Panzer IV, is one of the most iconic tanks of World War II, representing the backbone of the German armoured divisions during the conflict. Developed from the mid-1930s, the Panzer IV was initially conceived as an infantry support tank, intended to work alongside the lighter Panzer III, whose main role was to engage enemy armoured vehicles. However, evolving war tactics and the increasing technological superiority of the adversaries transformed the Panzer IV into a multi-purpose machine, continuously upgraded to remain competitive on the battlefield.

Produced in over 8,500 units between 1937 and 1945, the Panzer IV was used on all the main fronts of the conflict, from the North African desert to the Russian steppes, demonstrating extraordinary versatility and a unique ability to adapt to different roles and situations. The numerous variants of the tank, classified from Ausf. A to Ausf. J, reflect this evolution, including improvements in armament, armour and mobility.

Although it was gradually overtaken by more modern Allied tanks, such as the Soviet T-34 and the US Sherman, the Panzer IV remained in service until the end of the war due to its mechanical reliability and relative simplicity of production. Its historical and technological impact made it a symbol of German military power and a subject of great interest to scholars and military history enthusiasts.

▲ May 1940: A Panzerkampfwagen IV, version A, of the 9th Panzer Division during the advance through the Netherlands, presumably near Moerdijk. The number '432' on the turret indicates the 4th company, 3rd platoon, 2nd tank. A DKW SB350 motorbike of the Wehrmacht is parked in the foreground.

▲ Early versions of the Panzer IV (here Ausf. D) had a design very similar to that of the Panzerkampfwagen III.

■ DEVELOPMENT

The Panzer IV was born in a context where Germany was rebuilding its armed forces under the Nazi regime, violating the restrictions imposed by the Treaty of Versailles. In 1934, the German Army (Heer) began planning the creation of a modern armoured force that could support its military doctrine based on Blitzkrieg, or blitzkrieg. In this vision, tanks would have distinct and complementary roles. The Panzer III would be the main tank fighter, while the Panzer IV, initially designated the 'Bataillonsführerwagen' (battalion commander's vehicle), would provide direct infantry support and neutralise fortified enemy positions.

In 1935, Krupp received the contract to design the Panzer IV. The initial prototype, designated Ausf. A, was completed in 1936. This model was equipped with a 75 mm KwK 37 L/24 short gun, specifically designed to launch high explosive (HE) projectiles rather than penetrating ones. The armour was relatively thin, with a maximum thickness of 15 mm, sufficient against light weapons but vulnerable to the most powerful anti-tank guns of the time.

As the war progressed and more sophisticated threats emerged, the Panzer IV was continually modified to meet new challenges. From the Ausf. C onwards, the thickness of the armour was gradually increased. The introduction of the Panzer IV Ausf. F2 in 1942 represented a turning point: the short gun was replaced with the more powerful 75 mm KwK 40 L/43, capable of penetrating the armour of enemy tanks such as the Soviet T-34 and KV-1. This version transformed the Panzer IV into a main battle tank, suitable for both infantry support and direct confrontation with enemy vehicles.

At the same time, the design of the Panzer IV was optimised to simplify production and reduce costs. From the Ausf. H onwards, elements such as the Schutzpanzerungen, additional armoured panels mounted on the sides of the hull and turret, were introduced to improve protection against armour-piercing bullets and rockets. The frontal armour reached a thickness of 80 mm, greatly increasing the vehicle's survivability on the battlefield. However, these improvements made the tank heavier and less manoeuvrable, slightly reducing its speed and agility.

▲▼ Panzer IV assembly lines: the remarkable success and the large number of wagons produced of this model meant that production was well organised across several factories throughout the Reich. In these two pictures (one view from above) of the Nibelungenwerk workshops in the town of Sankt Valentin in Lower Austria.

▲ A Panzer IV Ausf. A performing a water-crossing demonstration exercise while being observed by Wehrmacht officers. (Bundesarchiv).

The production capabilities of the Panzer IV were another crucial element in its success. Unlike more advanced vehicles such as the Tiger or Panther, which required complex and expensive manufacturing processes, the Panzer IV was relatively simple to build and maintain. This enabled its large-scale production, making it the largest German tank of the war, with over 8,500 units built between 1937 and 1945.

The development of the Panzer IV was not only limited to the main tank: many specialised variants were introduced to meet specific needs. These included the Sturmpanzer IV, an assault howitzer used to bomb enemy positions, and the Flakpanzer IV, an anti-aircraft platform mounted on the hull of the Panzer IV. These modifications highlight the flexibility of the design and its ability to adapt to a wide range of battlefield roles.

Ultimately, the Panzer IV represented a perfect balance between power, reliability and the ability to evolve, becoming a symbol of the mechanisation of war and a key element of German military operations.

■ TECHNICAL SPECIFICATIONS

The Panzerkampfwagen IV, designed to fulfil a variety of roles on the battlefield, was a masterpiece of military engineering for its time. Its technical characteristics were continuously improved over the course of production, allowing it to remain effective against a rapidly changing war landscape. Below is an in-depth analysis of its main components.

Hull and turret

The hull of the Panzer IV was of conventional design, with a rectangular structure constructed from welded or riveted steel plates, depending on the variant. Early versions, such as the Ausf. A, had frontal armour of only 15 mm, sufficient against small arms. However, with the introduction of later variants, the armour thickness was gradually increased, reaching 80 mm in the Ausf. H.

The turret, mounted on a wide pivot ring, allowed 360 degrees of movement and housed the main gun and a coaxial machine gun. It was operated manually or by an electric system, with rotation speed varying depending on the version. The turret offered space for three crew members: the commander, gunner and servant.

Armament
The main gun of the Panzer IV varied significantly in the course of production.
- **KwK 37 L/24 (Ausf. A-F1):** This short 75 mm cannon was primarily designed for infantry support, using high explosive (HE) ammunition to destroy light fortifications and enemy positions.
- **KwK 40 L/43 and L/48 (Ausf. F2-J):** With the introduction of these versions, the Panzer IV became a versatile tank suitable for combat against other armoured vehicles. These guns, with a higher muzzle velocity, were able to penetrate the armour of Allied tanks, including the Soviet T-34 and the US Sherman.

In addition to the main gun, the Panzer IV was equipped with 7.92 mm MG 34 machine guns, mounted coaxially and in the hull for close-in defence against infantry.

Armour plating
The protection of the Panzer IV was one of the most improved aspects during its evolution:
- The first versions (Ausf. A-D) had frontal armour of 15-30 mm and lateral armour of 10-15 mm, vulnerable to medium-power anti-tank weapons.
- With the introduction of the Ausf. F and subsequent versions, the thickness was increased to 50 mm at the front, with additional armoured panels to protect the side surfaces.

▼ Starting with the Ausf. D, all Panzer IV tanks received the 300 hp Maybach engine also used in the Panzer III.

- The Ausf. H and Ausf. J saw the adoption of appliqué armour and side shields (Schürzen) to improve resistance against armour-piercing projectiles and rockets such as the British PIAT and US Bazooka.

Propulsion and mobility

The Panzer IV was powered by a Maybach engine, which varied slightly in power between the different versions:
- **Maybach HL 108 TR:** Used in early versions, this engine provided 250 hp.
- **Maybach HL 120 TRM:** fitted from the Ausf. E onwards, it increased power to 300 hp, improving overall performance.

The transmission was manual, with six or seven forward and one reverse gear, depending on the version. The top speed on the road varied between 38 and 42 km/h, while off-road it was around 15 to 20 km/h. The suspension was of the semi-elliptical leaf spring type, a simple and reliable choice, although it did not offer the same ride quality as the more advanced systems such as torsion bars used on other tanks. The Panzer IV's relatively low ground pressure allowed it excellent mobility over moderately difficult terrain, although it suffered in deep mud or snowy conditions.

Electronics and Internal Systems

The Panzer IV was equipped with a FuG 5 radio system, standard for German armoured units. This system allowed for effective communications between the vehicles and higher commands, providing an important tactical advantage. The internal layout was well organised to allow quick access to ammunition and instruments, improving crew efficiency.

Crew

The crew of Panzer IV consisted of five members:

▲ A Panzer IV Ausf. F1 with short barrel, displayed in the yards of the Nibelungenwerk workshops.

- **Commander:** Responsible for coordination and observation.
- **Gunner:** Aiming and firing the main cannon.
- **Loader:** Responsible for loading the cannon.
- **Pilot:** Positioned in the left front hull, manoeuvred the vehicle.
- **Radio operator/mitre gunner:** Handled communications and the machine gun mounted in the hull.

The crew layout was designed to maximise operational efficiency and ensure good synergy between roles.

Variants and customisation

The flexible design of the Panzer IV allowed the creation of numerous specialised variants, adapted to different scenarios:
- **Sturmpanzer IV (Brummbär):** Assault howitzer with a 150 mm cannon for destroying fortifications.
- **Flakpanzer IV (Wirbelwind and Ostwind):** Anti-aircraft versions armed with 20 mm or 37 mm automatic cannons.
- **Jagdpanzer IV:** Tank destroyer with a 75 mm long-range gun, mounted on a fixed superstructure.

Defects and Limitations

Despite its many qualities, the Panzer IV was not without its faults:
- **Increasing weight:** With increasing armour and armament, the weight of the vehicle increased to over 25 tonnes, reducing its speed and manoeuvrability.
- **Dated design:** Towards the end of the war, the Panzer IV was surpassed by more modern tanks such as the Soviet T-34/85 and the US Pershing.
- **Lateral Vulnerability:** Despite the improvements, the vehicle's flanks remained relatively weak against heavy weapons.

▲ Close-up of a slightly damaged tower. Of the two panoramic openings, currently closed, the one on the right was omitted in later versions. Small photo: mouth brake mounted on the Ausf. G.

▲ September 1939, invasion of Poland. Two Panzer IV tanks, model A, passing through a village. Bundesarchiv.

▼ Panzer IV Ausf. A parade through the streets of Komotau, in the Sudetenland region that had just been annexed by Germany in 1938. Bundesarchiv wiki CC3.

VERSIONS OF THE VEHICLE

The Panzer IV underwent significant evolution during World War II, with versions developed to improve armament, armour and mobility in response to increasing enemy challenges. The versions, identified by the initials 'Ausführung' (abbreviated to 'Ausf.'), are described here in chronological order.

■ Panzer IV Ausf. A (1936-1937): the first model

The Panzer IV Ausf. A, produced from 1937, represented the first version of the tank. With 14.5 mm armour on the hull and 20 mm on the turret, the Panzer IV Ausf. A was well protected against small calibre, but already showed its limitations against heavier enemy tanks. The 7.5 cm KwK 37 L/24 gun was useful against infantry and light vehicles, but was ineffective against armoured tanks.

- **Armament:** 75 mm KwK 37 L/24 short cannon, designed for high explosive (HE) ammunition.
- **Armour plating**: 15 mm maximum, only sufficient against light weapons.
- **Engine:** Maybach HL 108 TR with 250 hp.
- **Production:** Only 35 units were built, mainly for testing and training.

This version served as the basis for later improvements.

■ Panzer IV Ausf. B-C (1938-1939): improvements to mobility and protection

The later versions, Ausf. B and C, were produced in 1938 and 1939 respectively. The Ausf. B saw the introduction of new suspension and a slight correction of the structural defects present in the A model. Although the armour remained similar, the introduction of a wider turret and revised suspension system improved mobility, one of the key aspects of manoeuvre warfare. The Panzer IV Ausf. C, produced in 1939, continued this line of evolution, with armour reinforced to 30 mm at the front, making the vehicle more resistant against light artillery shells.

▲ A Panzer IV ausf. A bogged down near a destroyed bridge in Russia (Bundesarchiv).

Panzer IV Ausf. B

The Ausf. B introduced some improvements over the A version:
- **Armouring:** Increased to 20 mm on the front.
- **Engine:** The same Maybach HL 108 TR, but with an improved transmission.
- **Production:** 42 units.

This version was used in combat during the early stages of the war, including the Polish Campaign.

Panzer IV Ausf. C

The Ausf. C represented a further step forward in production:
- **Armour plating:** Front increased to 30 mm, with increased resistance to armour-piercing bullets.
- **Production:** 134 units.

This model participated in the invasion of France in 1940, showing some vulnerability to Allied anti-tank guns.

▲ Panzer IV Ausf. C, 1943.

▼ German medium tank Panzer IV Ausf. J, with Finnish marks, exhibited in the Finnish Tank Museum (Panssarimuseum) in Parola.

▲ German tank Panzer IV Ausf. D with its full crew filmed during a break in the spring of 1940 in France (Bundesarchiv).

■ Panzer IV Ausf. D-E (1940-1941): the start of experimentation with firepower

In 1940, the Ausf. D represented a major evolution of the Panzer IV, with the introduction of a more powerful engine and improved visibility capabilities for the crew. The new, higher turret allowed for greater gun elevation, while the main armament, the 7.5 cm KwK 37, was upgraded to improve accuracy. The Ausf. D proved an important step, but the growing threat posed by Soviet tanks and heavier allies such as the British Churchill forced the Wehrmacht to consider new modifications. In 1941, the Ausf. E offered further improvements, including further enhanced front armour and a greater ability to operate in difficult terrain, such as in Russia, where the war was intensifying.

Panzer IV Ausf. D (1939-1940)

With the Ausf. D, the Panzer IV began to show a more mature design:
- **Armour:** Reinforced on the sides and back.
- **Secondary armament:** Improvements in MG 34 machine gun arrangement.
- **Production:** 229 units.

It was widely employed during the French Campaign and operations in the Balkans.

Panzer IV Ausf. E (1940-1941)

The Ausf. E introduced further improvements that increased the effectiveness of the vehicle:
- **Armouring:** Increase to 50 mm on the front by adding welded plates.
- **Engine:** Maybach HL 120 TRM with 300 hp, improving speed and reliability.
- **Production:** 223 units.

This version saw service during Operation Barbarossa.

■ Panzer IV Ausf. F (1942): the anti-tank weapon begins to take shape

The real turning point for the Panzer IV came in 1942, with the introduction of the Ausf. F. This model marked a crucial transition, as the main armament was upgraded with the 7.5 cm KwK 40 L/43 gun, a significantly more powerful weapon capable of penetrating thicker enemy armour. This change proved vital in the fight against the Soviet T-34 and KV-1 tanks, which had rendered many previous German tanks obsolete. The Panzer IV Ausf. F, with its more powerful gun, thus became a real threat to enemy infantry and vehicles. The turret and armour were also further reinforced to resist new threats.

Panzer IV Ausf. F (1941-1942)

The Ausf. F was an important turning point:
- **Corrugation:** Further enhanced to 50 mm on all vertical surfaces.
- **Versions:** The Ausf. F was produced in two sub-variants:
    - **F1:** Still fitted with KwK 37 L/24.
    - **F2:** Equipped with the KwK 40 L/43, a 75 mm long gun capable of dealing effectively with Soviet T-34s.
- **Production:** 462 units (175 F1 and 287 F2).

The Ausf. F2 marked the transition of the Panzer IV to a main battle tank.

■ Panzer IV Ausf. G-H (1942-1943): integration with new requirements

The G version, introduced in 1942, brought a number of further modifications, including the addition of side armour and improvements to the suspension system, which increased the vehicle's stability. However, the challenges of war were growing, and the H version, introduced in 1943, saw further improvements adopted to deal with the new Allied tanks and air threats. The front armour was further reinforced, and the visibility system improved to allow commanders to see better on the battlefield. The Ausf. H represented the most productive version of the Panzer IV, with numerous examples built to support Wehrmacht operations on the Eastern Front and in North Africa.

PROTOTYPE PANZER IV AUSF. A TANK

▲ Panzer IV Ausf. A prototype - Germany, 1938.

Panzer IV Ausf. G (1942-1943)
The Ausf. G represented another step forward in armament and protection:
- **Cannon:** Long 75 mm KwK 40 L/43, later replaced with the L/48 for greater penetration.
- **Armouring:** Increased up to 80 mm at the front.
- **Production:** Approximately 1,700 units.

This version was widely used both on the Eastern Front and in North Africa.

Panzer IV Ausf. H (1943-1944)
The Ausf. H was the most produced version and one of the most robust models:
- **Armour plating:** Addition of Schürzen (side shields) for protection against light armour-piercing weapons and anti-tank rockets.
- **Engine:** The same Maybach HL 120 TRM, but the greater weight reduced mobility slightly.
- **Production:** Over 3,700 units.

The Ausf. H was the mainstay of the German armoured divisions in the second half of the war.

Panzer IV Ausf. J (1944-1945): simplification in response to the crisis
At the end of 1943, Germany faced a severe shortage of resources, and tank production had to be simplified. The J version, the last of the Panzer IV, was designed with the intention of reducing costs and speeding up production. Some of the more advanced features were eliminated, such as removable armour and some of the electronic complexities. Despite the reductions in technological capabilities, the Ausf. J represented the last manifestation of a tank that had played a crucial role throughout the war.

Panzer IV Ausf. J (1944-1945)
The Ausf. J was the last variant produced, simplified to reduce production costs:
- **Turret rotation system:** The electric motor was removed, leaving only a manual mechanism.
- **Armour:** Remained similar to the Ausf. H, with some minor modifications.
- **Production:** Around 3,100 units.

Despite being less sophisticated, the Ausf. J was essential in supporting the German war effort until the end of the war.

SPECIALISED VARIANTS
The Panzer IV was the basis for numerous variants designed for specific tasks:
- **Sturmpanzer IV (Brummbär):** Equipped with a 150 mm howitzer for attacks against fortifications.
- **Flakpanzer IV:** Anti-aircraft versions such as the Wirbelwind (with four 20 mm cannons) and the Ostwind (with a 37 mm cannon).
- **Jagdpanzer IV:** Tank destroyer armed with a 75 mm L/70 cannon mounted on a modified hull.
- **Munitionsschlepper:** ammunition transport vehicle.
- **Bergepanzer IV:** Recovery vehicle based on the hull of the Panzer IV.

Conclusion: a model that has stood the test of time
All in all, the Panzer IV not only represented one of the Wehrmacht's most successful platforms, but also one of the greatest examples of technological and tactical adaptation during the Second World War. From its origins as an infantry carrier, the Panzer IV developed into a versatile tank capable of dealing with any kind of threat. Although later versions could not compete with heavier vehicles such as the Tiger, the Panzer IV remained at the forefront throughout the war, demonstrating a remarkable ability to evolve and respond to the changing demands of the conflict.

PANZER IV AUSF. B TANK, POLAND 1939

▲ Panzer IV Ausf. B (Vs. Kfz. 622), Panzer-Brigade 8, 5th Panzer-Division, Opatów, Poland, September 1939: the second produced version of the Panzer IV, the Ausf. B was armed with the 7.5 cm KwK 37 L/24 short gun, designed for infantry support. During the Polish campaign, this model represented an innovative component of the Blitzkrieg, offering effective fire support through its ability to destroy light fortifications and enemy troops. However, it was equipped with relatively thin armour, making it vulnerable to more modern anti-tank projectiles.

▲ Ausf. E on the march during the victorious advance into the Soviet Union in the summer of 1941.

▼ Panzer IV Ausf. F parked in a Ukrainian village.

▲ Panzer IV B passes through a French village under the curious eyes of the inhabitants. France, 1944 (Bundesarchiv).

▼ A PzKpfw IV Ausf. H of the 12th Panzer Division operating on the Eastern Front in the USSR, 1944.

PANZER IV AUSF. C TANK, FRANCE 1940

▲ Panzer IV Ausf. C of the 6th Company, 2nd Battalion of Panzer-Regiment 15, 8th Panzer-Brigade, 5th Panzer-Division, France, June 1940.

OPERATIONAL USE

The operational deployment of the Panzer IV during the Second World War was a crucial aspect of the success of the German armed forces, particularly in the early stages of the conflict, but also during the following years as the Panzer IV adapted to the increasingly complex demands of warfare and the growing power of enemy tanks. Here we will examine in detail how the Panzer IV was used in the various theatres of battle, its modifications during the conflict and the operational challenges it faced.

■ THE BLITZKRIEG AND THE FRENCH CAMPAIGN (1940)

The Panzer IV proved pivotal during the French Campaign, where it was employed as an integral part of the German panzer forces in the famous 'Blitzkrieg'. The tank, together with the Panzer III, formed the backbone of the German armoured forces, but it was above all the Panzer IV that emerged as the most versatile and reliable vehicle in this early phase of the war.

The main role of the Panzer IV in France was to support infantry forces and penetrate enemy defences. Its mobility, combined with its ability to destroy enemy fortifications and infantry groups, made it ideal for deep operations and the occupation of enemy positions. However, despite its importance, the Panzer IV was not able to deal effectively with Allied tanks, such as the French Char B1, but distinguished itself in infantry support operations and in combat against soft-skinned targets (without armoured protection).

■ OPERATION BARBAROSSA (1941)

The invasion of the Soviet Union in the summer of 1941 marked a significant change in the operational deployment of the Panzer IV. During Operation Barbarossa, the Panzer IV was involved in large-scale combat against the Red Army, particularly during the first months of the invasion. The German tank proved effective against poorly equipped Soviet forces, but the increasing presence of Soviet tanks, such as the T-34 and KV-1, highlighted the limitations of the Panzer IV, which was initially unable to effectively counter Soviet heavy tanks.

▲ Russian infantry in winter camouflage in front of Panzer IV with turret and side skirts (Bundesarchiv).

Despite the difficulties, the Panzer IV continued to play a leading role in tank battles, both in attack and defence. The armament of the 7.5 cm KwK 40 L/43 cannon, mounted on later versions of the Panzer IV, allowed the tank to be more competitive against the Soviet T-34s, although it was still unable to easily destroy them at longer ranges. Its mobility and ability to adapt to difficult terrain made it a useful weapon for outflanking manoeuvres and support actions.

■ THE NORTH AFRICAN CAMPAIGN (1941-1943)

The Panzer IV also played a crucial role in the North African Campaign, where it was deployed alongside Afrikakorps forces under the command of Field Marshal Erwin Rommel. Initially, the Panzer IVs present in North Africa belonged to the Ausf. D and E variants, armed with the KwK 37 L/24. These proved effective against infantry and light fortifications, but suffered against the British Matilda II tanks, whose armour was difficult to penetrate.

The situation improved with the introduction of the Ausf. F2 variants, equipped with the KwK 40 L/43 gun, which allowed the Panzer IVs to effectively face the British Crusader and American Grant and Sherman tanks. Tactical superiority and the ability to co-ordinate artillery and air support allowed the Panzer IVs to achieve significant victories, such as at Gazala and Tobruk in 1942. However, increasing logistical pressure and Allied numerical superiority led to the defeat of the Axis forces in North Africa in 1943.

The battles in the desert highlighted both the strengths and weaknesses of the Panzer IV. The tank proved superior to the Allied vehicles in terms of manoeuvrability and the ability to strike accurately at medium distances. However, the extreme climate of the desert imposed constant maintenance and accelerated consumption of resources such as air filters and fuel, putting a strain on German logistics.

▲ Panzer IV column advances into the sandy roads of North Africa.

PANZER IV AUSF. D, FRANCE 1940

▲ Panzer IV Ausf. D of the 4th Company, I. Battalion of Panzer-Regiment 7, 4th Panzer-Brigade, 10th Panzer-Division, France, May 1940.

▲ Column of Finnish Panzer IV Ausf. J at Tuira, Oulu, Finland, in November 1944.

▼ Panzer IV tank of the 4th Armoured Division (Panzer Regiment 35) with protective skirts on the turret (marked with the number 135). In addition to the crew, as usual, the vehicle was also used by the infantry.

PANZER IV AUSF. E TANK, SOVIET UNION 1941

▲ Panzer IV Ausf. E of the 4th Company, I. Battalion of Panzer-Regiment 3, 2nd Panzer-Division, Soviet Union, July 1941.

■ PANZER IV ON THE EASTERN FRONT (1942-1944)

As the conflict on the Eastern Front intensified, the Panzer IV continued to be the main tank of the German armoured forces, even though its ability to counter more modern Soviet tanks, such as the T-34/85 and IS-2, was severely tested. During the Battle of Stalingrad (1942-1943) and the subsequent Soviet offensive, the Panzer IV faced the Soviet forces in fierce battles.

Its ability to maintain a certain effectiveness in tank battles, thanks to the evolution of its armament and protection, continued to make it useful in defensive and containment operations. Versions equipped with a 7.5 cm KwK 40 L/48 cannon were better able to take on the T-34s, but the increasing number of Soviet tanks and the numerical superiority of the Russians led to heavy losses for the Wehrmacht.

■ ITALY AND THE MEDITERRANEAN THEATRE (1943-1945)

With the invasion of Sicily in July 1943 and the subsequent Allied advance into the Italian peninsula, the Panzer IV was deployed to slow the enemy advance. The Ausf. H version, with its reinforced armour and side shields, was particularly suitable for defending mountain passes and fortified positions.

German armoured units employed the Panzer IV in decisive battles such as Cassino and Anzio, where the rugged terrain and climatic conditions often limited the effectiveness of the armoured vehicles. Despite its increasing obsolescence compared to Allied tanks, the Panzer IV continued to pose a significant threat due to its versatility and ability to support infantry in defensive operations.

In Italy, the use of the Panzer IV focused on rearguard actions and mobile defence, taking advantage of the difficult terrain to slow down Allied forces. Ambushes and night operations became common tactics to maximise the effectiveness of the tanks. However, the arrival of Allied heavy vehicles, such as the Churchill and early M26 Pershing, posed increasing challenges.

▲ Panzer IV number 813 overloaded with troops in operation during the Italian campaign.

PANZER IV AUSF. F TANK, SOVIET UNION, JUNE 1941

▲ Panzer IV Ausf. F of the 4th Company, I. Battalion of Panzer-Regiment 31, 5th Panzer-Division, Soviet Union, June 1941.

▲ Balkan Campaign, Greece 1941 - Panzer IV (turret number 713) with crew.

▼ South of Russia (Ukraine): two Panzer IV tanks with side guns on a heavily muddy road, typical of the theatre in the East.

PANZER IV AUSF. F1 TANK

▲ Panzer IV Ausf. F1 (7.5 cm) Sd.Kfz. 161: version armed with the 7.5 cm KwK 37 L/24 short gun, designed for infantry support and employed in the early years of World War II.

THE PANZER IV IN DEFENCE COMBAT (1943-1945)

As the war evolved and Allied attacks intensified on various fronts, the Panzer IV was progressively used more frequently in defensive roles, rather than in attack operations. Its capabilities, unfortunately, were no longer in step with Allied tanks such as the Sherman M4 and T-34/85, which had superior armament and greater mobility. Nevertheless, the Panzer IV continued to play a crucial role in the defence of cities, fortified lines and in some containment operations.

Versions of the Panzer IV with reinforced armour and improved firing systems were used in urban battles, such as those that took place during the Allied occupation of Germany, and in defence against the Red Army. Although it was not able to counter the new Allied tanks head-on, the Panzer IV continued to play a key role in supporting infantry units and in the limited offensive against opposing forces.

THE WESTERN FRONT (1944-1945)

With the Normandy landings in June 1944, the Panzer IV faced a new wave of Allied tanks, including the American Sherman and the British Churchill. Despite being surpassed in design by more modern tanks such as the Panther and Tiger, the Panzer IV continued to form the backbone of the German armoured divisions. Its presence was crucial to maintaining the operational capability of the armoured forces, although the Allies' numerical and air superiority made its deployment increasingly difficult.

▲ A British Crusader tank overtakes a burning German Panzer IV during Operation Crusader in the North African campaign in late 1941.

During the Battle of Normandy, the Panzer IV distinguished itself by its ability to effectively engage Allied tanks at medium range. However, its vulnerability to air strikes and modern anti-tank weapons, such as the American bazooka and the British PIAT, limited its overall effectiveness. Side shields (Schürzen) were specifically designed to deal with these threats but could not fully compensate for its weaknesses.

The final stages of the war saw the Panzer IV involved in the battles of the Siegfried Line and the Ardennes Offensive. In these operations, Panzer IV still proved to be a formidable opponent, but wear and tear, fuel shortages and increasing Allied pressure led to a rapid decline in its operational capabilities.

The decline of the German armoured forces was evident in 1945, when the Panzer IV was employed in desperate urban defence actions in Berlin and other cities. Despite serious shortcomings, the experience of the crews and the ability to exploit urban terrain allowed the Panzer IV to inflict significant losses on the Allies, even under unfavourable circumstances.

■ THE LAST PHASE OF PANZER IV (1944-1945)

The use of the Panzer IV in the final phase of the war focused mainly on Germany's inner defences and the eastern front lines, where it was employed in support roles and as a defensive vehicle against enemy forces. At this point, many of the more advanced versions of the Panzer IV were equipped with thicker armour, 7.5 cm KwK 42 L/70 guns and other modifications that sought to keep the tank competitive against Allied vehicles.

■ CONCLUSIONS ON THE DEPLOYMENT OF PANZER IV

Overall, the Panzer IV was one of the longest-lived tanks of the Second World War, deployed in numerous theatres of battle and adapted to various operational roles. Although it was never the most powerful or the most advanced of the Wehrmacht's tanks, its versatility and adaptability allowed it to continue to be a key element of German forces, even during the most critical periods of the war. Its ability to evolve in response to new challenges, from the first infantry support versions to the more powerful 7.5 cm L/70 gun versions, made it an essential tank, capable of maintaining a certain level of effectiveness even when the conflict took a turn for the worst for Germany.

STRENGTHS IN OPERATIONAL DEPLOYMENT

- **Versatility:** The Panzer IV could be used both as an infantry support vehicle and as an anti-tank combat tank, thanks to the numerous modifications made during the war.
- **Reliability:** Despite the difficult conditions, the Panzer IV proved generally reliable and easy to maintain compared to more complex models such as the Panther.
- **Adaptability:** The ability to mount additional equipment, such as Schürzen and improved cannons, enabled the Panzer IV to deal effectively with new threats on the battlefield.

LIMITATIONS IN OPERATIONAL USE

- **Vulnerability:** Despite improvements, the Panzer IV remained vulnerable to more modern tanks and heavy anti-tank weapons.
- **Increasing weight:** The increase in armour and armament progressively reduced the mobility of the vehicle.
- **Obsolescence:** Towards the end of the war, the Panzer IV was surpassed in terms of design by the new Allied and Soviet tanks.

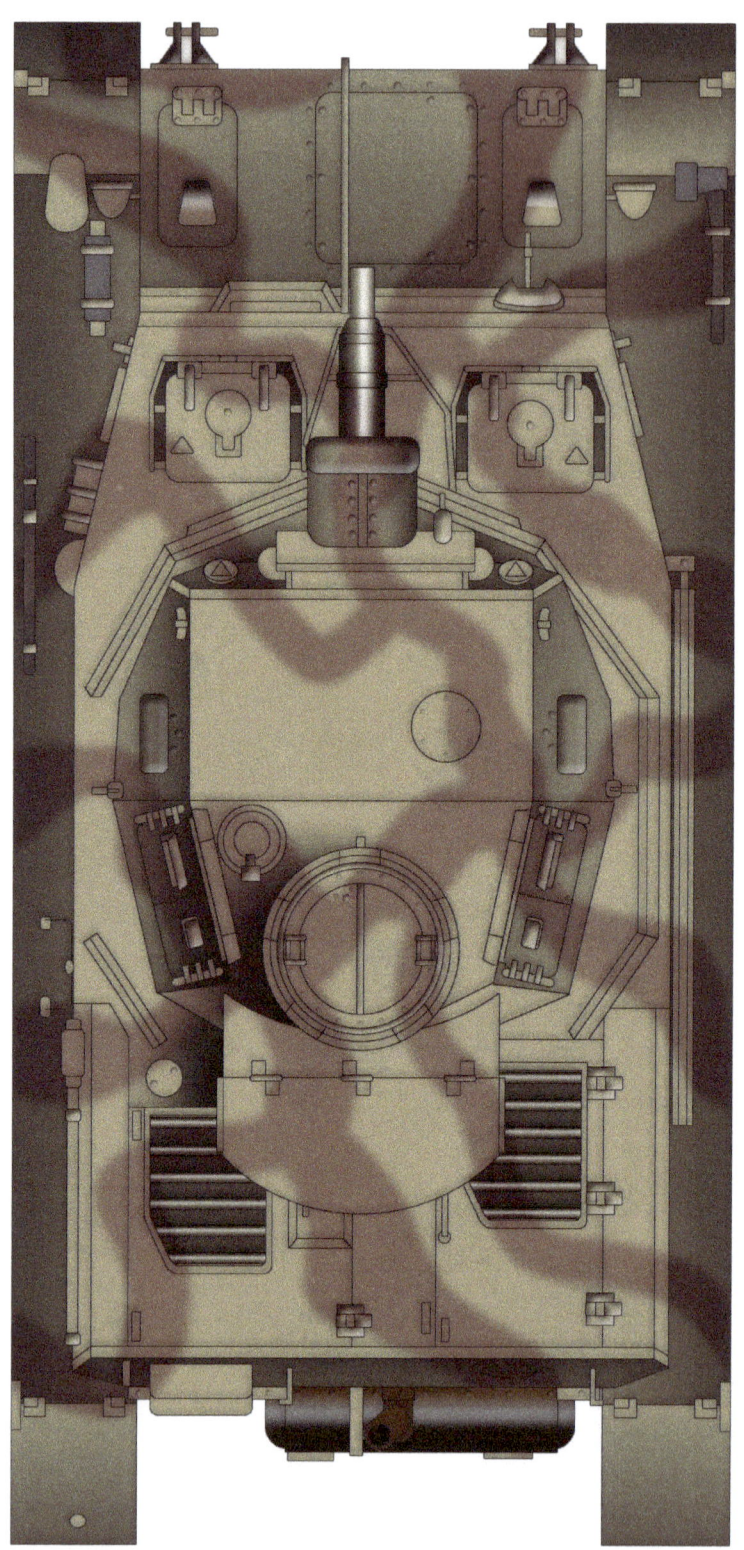

▲ Profile view from above of Panzer IV.

PANZER IV TANK AUSF. F2, EGYPT, OCTOBER 1942

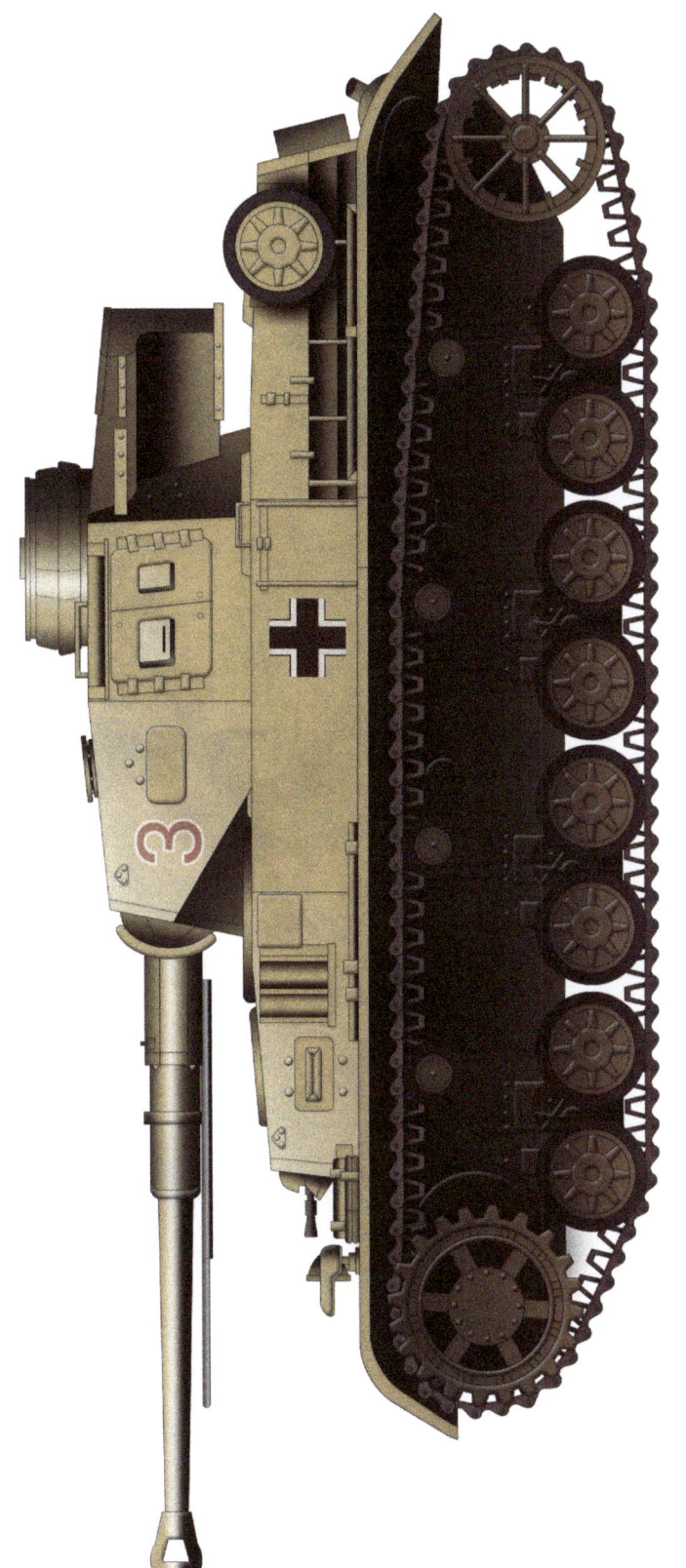

▲ Panzer IV Ausf. F2 of the 4th Panzer-Regiment 5, 21st Panzer-Division, El Alamein, Egypt, October 1942: version equipped with the 7.5 cm KwK 40 L/43 long gun, designed to take on enemy armoured vehicles. Used during the North African Campaign, the F2 model represented a significant improvement over previous variants due to its greater firepower and improved penetration capability.

▲ Russian Campaign: Panzer IV column crossing a water course.

▼ More modern versions of the Panzer IV were far superior to the T-34 until the introduction of the T34/85.

PANZER IV AUSF. F2 TANK, SUMMER 1942

▲ Panzer IV Ausf. F2 of the 3rd Company, 60th Infantry Division, Stalingrad suburbs, summer 1942: equipped with the 7.5 cm KwK 40 L/43 long gun, designed to effectively counter Soviet tanks. This model was employed during the siege of Stalingrad, demonstrating its technical superiority in the context of extremely intense urban and field combat.

▲ View of the Panzer IV tank from the front and back.

▲ Summer 1944, Normandy campaign, Panzer IV immobilised at St. Martin de Cenilly, France.

▼ Despite its conventional form, the Panzer IV was a powerful fighting vehicle.

PANZER IV SD.KFZ. 161

PANZER IV AUSF. G TANK, SOVIET UNION, JULY 1943

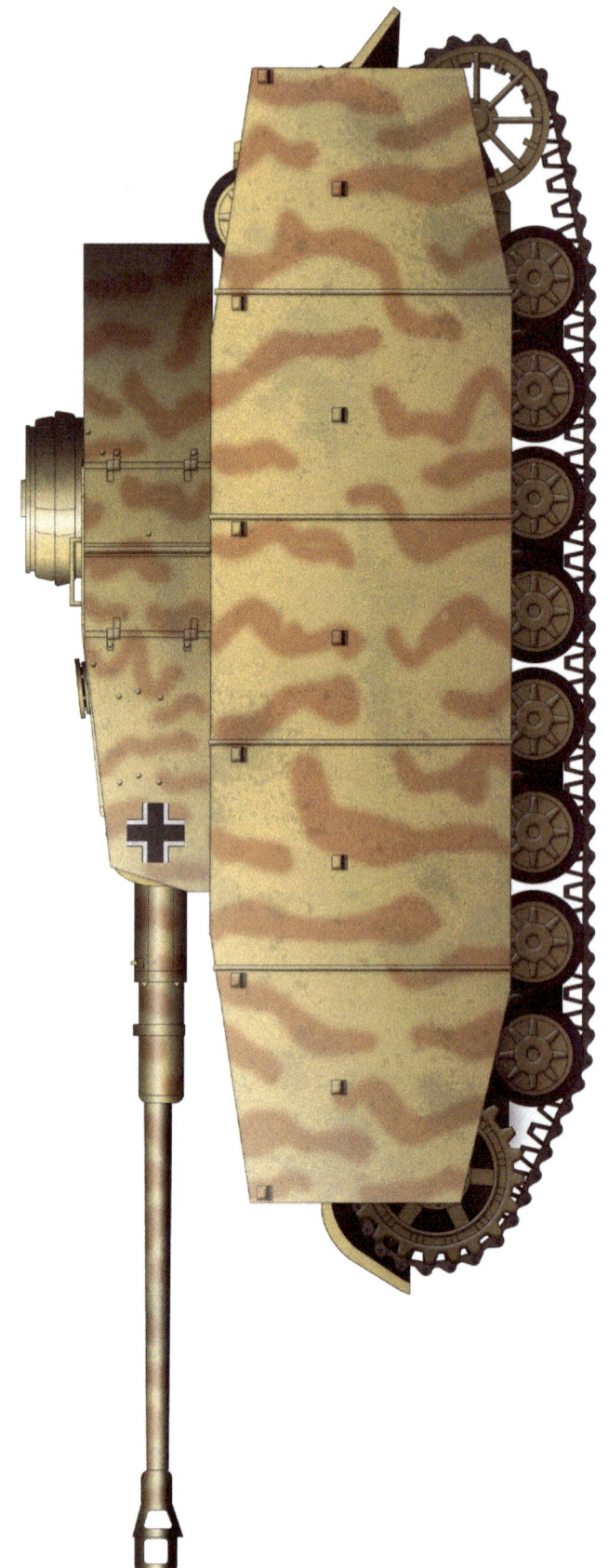

▲ Panzer IV Ausf. G of the 6th Company, II. Battalion of the Panzer-Regiment Leibstandarte SS Adolf Hitler, 1st SS-Panzer-Grenadier-Division 'Leibstandarte SS Adolf Hitler,' Soviet Union, Kursk sector, July 1943: equipped with the 7.5 cm KwK 40 L/48 gun, it was designed to face Soviet heavy tanks such as the T-34. During the Battle of Kursk, one of the largest armoured battles in history, the Panzer IV Ausf. G played a crucial role due to its combination of firepower, mobility and protection.

CAMOUFLAGE & MARKINGS

In the early stages of the war in Poland and France, the German army mainly used vehicles painted in Dunkelgrau (RAL 7021), with some vehicles also painted in Dunkelbraun (RAL 7017) as a camouflage (motif) until the Oberkommando des Heeres decided that only Dunkelgrau should be used. The decision affected not only tanks, but also all AFVs, including armored cars, half-tracks and even the mobile canteen vehicles were painted the same color.

This Dunkelgrau is often shown in illustrations incorrectly. The point is that it was in reality a very dark bluish-gray color. This error occurs due to the fact that gray tends to "blend" effectively with the surrounding colors and consequently appear much lighter.

The war, however, opened the eyes of Hitler's generals, especially in Russia and Africa, where both theaters of operation Dunkelgrau could be spotted miles away, a clear invitation to enemy fire. Therefore, German divisions in the USSR used any useful material to color their vehicles more effectively including natural materials such as chalk, bedding, piled snow until the inevitable whitewash was available. The resulting camouflage saved the lives of many tank crew. These ad hoc coverings also had the advantage that they gradually washed out with the late winter and the early spring rains. In Libya, although white was not needed, there was a lot of trouble in finding a good solution but with typical German thoroughness, eventually a solution was found ,when Gelbbraun (RAL 8000) was sent to the North African Front and the vehicles in Dunkelgrau were quickly recamouflaged with the desert colouring. In addition to coloring in Gelbraun, Graugrün (RAL 7008) was also used in Africa, the latter in different variants frequently conditioned by what the tankers had on hand, or what they managed to capture from the enemy.

Since 1942, official colors began to become scarce at the front and often at the factory as well. Military vehicles were therefore painted using alternative color schemes from whatever was available, especially for the desert vehicles which never received their full complement of supply, due to Allied naval and aircraft interdiction of supply convoys, however schemes using Braun (RAL 8020) and Grau (brown and gray, RAL 7027) were often met on the battlefield. In the pages of the book you will find as clear images as possible of these colors and their RAL designation. Apart from Africa, vehicles painted in the two-tone camouflage already in use in the desert also began to be used on the Eastern Front.

It should be remembered, however, that by mid-conflict most German tanks in Russia were still Dunkelgrau, at least until 1943, when the OKH issued a new order that the standard base color of all vehicles became Dunkelgelb (dark yellow, RAL 7028). The color was not a true yellow, but rather tended toward bronze. A delicate color anyway, which varied enormously, depending on many factors: who painted it, how much it was diluted with solvents, weather, wear and tear, etc. RAL 7028 offers, even in the bibliography, a large number of "variations". So it was partly by chance, partly by luck that they came up with that modern camouflage that the Germans called the *Hinterhalt-Tarnung* or "Ambush." A complicated

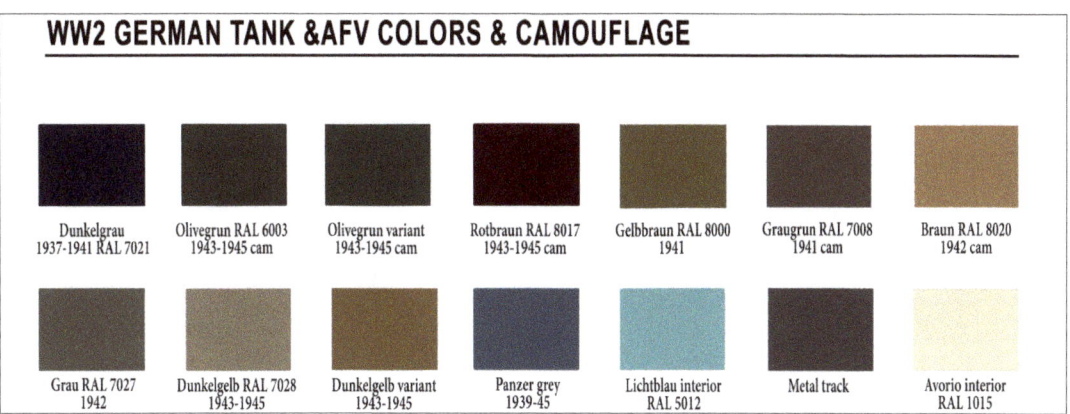

aspect to describe, but in fact it is an effect of light filtered through natural foliage, in short, a very effective camouflage.

Just as in works of art, one could also speak of styles, as varied as possible so that one was similar to that of the *pointillisme* of the French Impressionists, and another took the form of disc or mottled. The choice of one style or the other was also in a way the signature of the factory that produced the vehicles as from mid-1944 the vehicles were painted in the production plants. Factory-applied colors were a base of Dunkelgelb, with flecks of Rotbraun a red brown and Olivgrün an olive green. More and more problems arose with storage, thunderstorms and general events which made the outgoing supply varied.

Finally, in December 1944, a new order was issued that the tanks were to be painted all over with a base coat over the red-oxide primer consisting of Dunkelgrün and/or Olivgrün with applications of Dunkelgelb and Rotbraun stripes and spots, and this appears to be the last order given for camouflage while the war was in progress.

The application of camouflage was generally done with airborne paint sprays, failing which it was done "the old-fashioned way", using brushes, mops, or simply rags on the end of a stick. These techniques and the make do and mend attitude that typified later war German forces vastly increases the camouflage variations that would later be destined for the battlefield.

Like all armies, the German army understood from its vast battle experience that concealing vehicles in defensive or offensive postures would increase the odds of surviving the encounter. Therefore, in addition to camouflage painted on the vehicle itself, foliage (branches, bushes, hay, even woodpiles) was often used to cover the vehicle, usually from the front, to make it even more difficult to detect and distinguish from its surroundings. More rarely, tarpaulins and camouflage cloths and nets mixed with foliage were also used to further conceal the tank. Not least, mud and snow were also an inexpensive, but effective, camouflage that was very useful in blending in with the surroundings.

▲ The white identification crosses were removed after the invasion of Poland, after they were used by the enemy as a welcome aiming aid.

PANZER IV AUSF. G TANK, SOVIET UNION, WINTER 1942-1943

▲ Panzer IV Ausf. G (late production vehicle) of the 14th Panzer-Division, Stalingrad, winter 1942-1943: equipped with the 7.5 cm KwK 40 L/48 gun, an improved version compared to previous models, with additional armour to resist Soviet anti-tank shells.

▲ PzKpfw IV tank number 625 of the 12th SS-Panzer-Division Hitlerjugend in Normandy (Bundesarchiv).

▼ Campaign of Italy: crew of a Panzer IV (with turret skirts) (tank number 303) of the 16th Armoured Division, standing on the side of a road in 1944.

PANZER IV AUSF. G TANK, TUNISIA, SPRING 1943

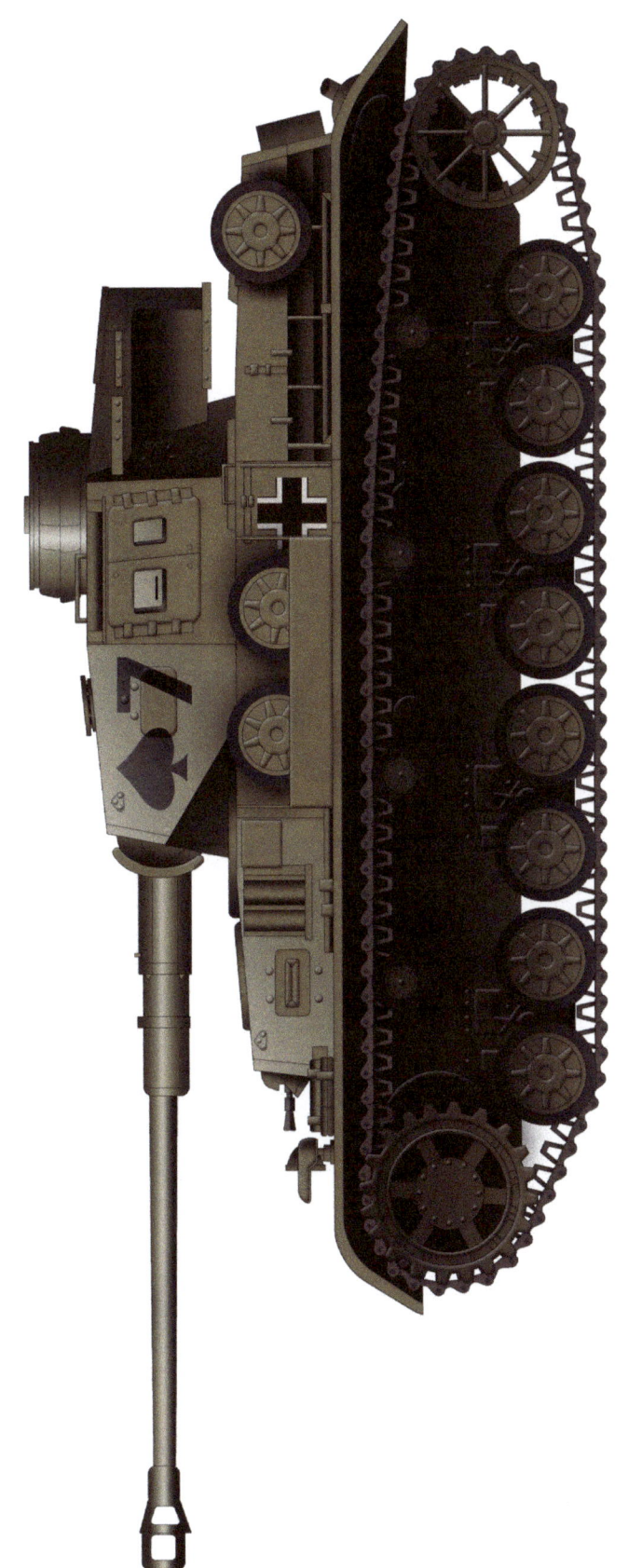

▲ Panzer IV Ausf. G, XVth Panzer-Division, Tunisia, spring 1943: late production vehicle, upgraded with the new 7.5 cm KwK 40 L/48 gun, which replaced the previous shorter gun, significantly improving penetration capability against Allied tanks. Deployed during the campaign in Tunisia, the Panzer IV Ausf. G represented an adaptation to the new requirements of the front, facing the Allied forces in a difficult and challenging desert environment.

PANZER IV AUSF. H TANK, ITALY, SEPTEMBER 1943

▲ Panzer IV Ausf. H (Sd.Kfz. 161/2), SS-Panzer-Regiment 1, SS-Panzer-Grenadier-Division 'Leibstandarte SS Adolf Hitler', Milan, Italy, September 1943: equipped with the 7.5 cm KwK 40 L/48 gun, the Ausf. H was an advanced version of the Panzer IV, with improvements to the armour and suspension system.

PRODUCTION AND EXPORT

Exports of the Panzer IV began mainly before the war, when Nazi Germany was trying to strengthen its alliances. The first country to acquire the Panzer IV was Spain, which used it to strengthen its army during the Spanish Civil War. Francisco Franco's Nationalist forces, which enjoyed the support of Fascist Germany, received several Panzer IVs, which were deployed against Republican forces. In this context, the Panzer IV proved its effectiveness in a conflict that saw the use of modern armoured vehicles.

With the start of the Second World War, Germany continued to use the Panzer IV to strengthen its alliances. In 1940, Bulgaria and Romania, both allies of Germany, received a few Panzer IVs. These tanks were mainly used in support operations, but their presence on the battlefields did not have as decisive an impact as the German forces. However, the supply of the Panzer IV to the Allied countries demonstrated Germany's desire to consolidate its dominance in Eastern Europe by supporting local forces with advanced equipment.

One of the most significant exports, however, was to Italy. The relationship between Italy and Germany during the Second World War also resulted in close cooperation in the military sector. The Panzer IV, in its various versions, was supplied in limited numbers to Italy, which used them mainly on the African front and during campaigns in Europe. Although the Italians had developed their own tanks, such as the L6/40 and AB 40/42 armoured cars, the Panzer IV became an important support, particularly in operations in North Africa, where its firepower and endurance were crucial against British tanks.

Other countries such as Finland also received Panzer IVs, although in more limited quantities, using them mainly in the war against the Soviet Union. Finland, which was initially neutral but later sided with Germany during the Continuation War (1941-1944), obtained some tanks as part of German support. These vehicles contributed to the Finnish defence against the Red Army, but the use of the Panzer IV was only one aspect of the Finnish strategy.

Overall, the export of the Panzer IV not only proved its effectiveness as a combat tank, but also its ability to adapt to various geopolitical scenarios. The countries that used it appreciated it for its performance in difficult terrain and dynamic warfare scenarios, but its limited production for export meant that it could never replace German forces on the battlefield. Nevertheless, the Panzer IV remained one of the most influential tanks of the war, not only because of its use by Germany, but also because of its adoption by allies and neutral countries.

Bulgaria
- It acquired 97 Panzer IVs (G and H versions) for the **Bronirana brigade** during World War II. The tanks were used in operations on the various fronts.

Czechoslovakia
- After the end of World War II, the Red Army recovered and stored numerous German armoured vehicles, including **165 Panzer IVs**. The Czechoslovak government obtained permission to use them, recovering another **102 Panzer IVs** from Soviet-occupied workshops.
- By 1947, the **Czechoslovak Army** had **245 Panzer IVs** in versions D, G, H, J. These tanks were repaired and redesignated as **T-40/75**, remaining in service until 1954, when they were replaced by Soviet T-34s.

Finland
- It obtained **15 Panzer IVs in 1944**, which were assigned to the **Panssaridivisioona** to reinforce its armoured capabilities.

Italy
- It received **12 Panzer IV Ausf. G** from Germany, employing them in the **1st 'M' Armoured Division**. After 8 September 1943, the division was disbanded and the tanks returned to German control.

Romania

- Between **1942 and 1944**, Romania acquired more than **116 Panzer IVs**, using them in the **Divizia 1 Blindată**. These tanks were used both in operations on the Eastern Front and in support of allied troops.

Syria

- In **1950**, France sold Syria **11 Panzer IVs**. Later, in **1955**, Syria bought **45 Panzer IVs** from Czechoslovakia.
- In **1965**, Syria received **17 Panzer IVs** from Spain. The tanks were involved in conflicts, including the **Six-Day War (1967)**, where they were destroyed or captured by Israel.

Slovakia

- After the Second World War, Czechoslovakia, having received German armoured material, included **Panzer IVs** in its equipment, using them in numerous defensive sectors.

Spain

- In **1943**, Spain bought **20 Panzer IV Ausf. H** from Germany. These tanks were used in the **'Brunete' División** until 1954, when they were replaced by US **M24 Chaffee** tanks.
- In **1965**, they were sold to Syria.

Hungary

- In **1942**, Hungary received **22 Panzer IV Ausf. F1** and **10 Panzer IV Ausf. F2**. The **Hungarian 1st Armoured Division** employed them on the Eastern Front, but these were destroyed during the **Soviet counteroffensive of 1943**.
- In 1944, the collaborationist Hungarian government received **12 Panzer IV Ausf. G** and **30 Panzer IV Ausf. H**, but these tanks did not survive to the end of the war.

▲ Positions of the crew members in a German Panzer IV Ausf.F2 tank. The driver (1) is seated in the vehicle hull at the front left, the radio operator (2) sits at the front right, the gunner (3) is seated in the turret to the left of the gun, the loader (4) is positioned to the right of the gun and the commander (5) is seated at the rear of the turret behind the gun.

▲ A Panzer IV Ausf. G '413' in desert colours, with the typical Afrika Korps palm-shaped insignia, with the inscription 'Friederike' in Fraktur lettering on the gun barrel next to the mantle.

▼ Panzer IV Ausf. J preserved in the Museum of the Slovak National Uprising in Banská Bystrica.

▲ Wreckage of a Panzer IV following the Battle of Tannenberg and remained there in the woods until the early 1950s.
▼ The wreckage of a Syrian Panzer IV abandoned in the Golan Heights, showing the longevity of this very successful tank!

PANZER IV AUSF. H TANK, VILLERS-BOCAGE, 13 JUNE 1944

▲ Panzer IV Ausf. H, 6th Company, II. Battalion, Panzer-Lehr-Regiment 130, Panzer-Lehr-Division, France, Normandy, Villers-Bocage, 13 June 1944: equipped with the 7.5 cm KwK 40 L/48 gun. Used during the Battle of Villers-Bocage, an important stage in Normandy, the German tank took part in the fighting against British forces in an urban and field combat environment. The Panzer-Lehr-Division, one of the most experienced and best equipped formations, employed the Panzer IV as one of its main offensive tools.

DATA SHEET PANZER IV SD.KFZ. 161

	Ausf. A-B-C	Ausf. D-E	Ausf. F	Ausf. G	Ausf. H	Ausf. J
Overall size						
Weight	17,7 t / C: 18,5 t	20 t / E: 21 t	22,3 t / F2: 23,6 t	23,6 t	25 t	=
Length	5,87 m	5,92 m	5,92 m (F2: 6,63)	6,63 m	7,02 m	=
Width	2,83 m	2,84 m	2,88 m	=	=	=
Height	2,85 m	2,68 m	=	=	=	=
Armament						
Main armament	7,5-cm-KwK 37	7,5-cm-KwK 37	= (F2: KwK 40 L/43 da 7,5 cm)	7,5-cm-KwK 40	7,5-cm-KwK 40	7,5-cm-KwK 40
Calibre length (KwK)	L/24	L/24	L/24 (F2: L/43)	L/43	L/48	L/48
Barrel length (KwK)	1,80 m	1,80 m	1,80 m (F2: 3,22 m)	3,22 m	3,60 m	3,60 m
Barrel life	13.000 rounds	=	13.000 colpi (F2: 6.000)	6.000 rounds	=	=
Secondary armament	1 MG 34	2 MG 34	=	=	=	=
Ammunition	KwK: 80 / MG: 2700	=	KwK: 80 (F2: 87) / MG: 3150	KwK: 87 / MG: 3150	=	=
Armour						
Front hull	30 mm/80°	30 mm/80° (E: 30 + 30 mm)	50 mm/80°	=	80 mm/80°	=
Side hull	15 mm/90°	20 mm/90° (E: 20 + 20 mm)	30 mm/90°	=	=	=
Back hull	15 mm/80-90°	20 mm/80-90°	=	=	=	=
Hull top	10 mm	=	=	=	=	=
Hull bridge	10 mm	=	=	=	=	=
Front turret	20 mm/80° (C: 30 mm)	30 mm/80°	50 mm/80°	=	=	=
Side turret	20 mm/65°	=	30 mm/65°	=	=	=
Rear turret	20 mm/75°	=	30 mm/75°	=	=	=
Turret top	10 mm	=	=	=	16-25 mm	=
Mobility						
Engine (Maybach)	HL 120 TR Water-cooled 12-cylinder petrol engine	=	=	=	=	=
Power per min^{-1}	300 PS (220 kW)/3000	=	=	=	=	=
Cylinders	11,87 L	=	=	=	=	=
Gearbox	6 / 1	=	=	=	=	=
Max. speed	40 km/h	=	=	=	=	=
Reserve	470 l	=	=	=	=	680 l
Autonomy	200 km (road) / 130 (elsewhere)	=	=	=	=	300 km (road) / 180 (elsewhere)
Track width	38 cm	=	40 cm	=	=	=

▲ The ammunition carrier at the rear of the tank could carry three of these 60 cm grenades.

PANZER IV AUSF. J TANK

▲ Panzer IV Ausf. J (7.5 cm KwK 40 L/48) (Sd.Kfz. 161/2): the last produced version of the Panzer IV, equipped with the 7.5 cm KwK 40 L/48 gun, which offered good penetration capability compared to previous models. The Ausf. J was equipped with reinforced armour and production simplifications to cope with the logistical difficulties at the end of the war. Among the most noticeable changes were the reduced equipment and the absence of certain devices, such as the commander's visor. This vehicle was mainly used in 1944-1945, during the final stages of the conflict, on both the Eastern and Western fronts.

▲ Panzer IV tank and crew of the German 12th SS Panzer Division in Belgium and France, 1943.

▼ Panzer IV driven to the rear by American GIs. The vehicle was captured intact during the battle of Grandvillers, France on 18 October 1944. Signal US archives.

PANZER IV TANK AUSF. J, LITHUANIA, OCTOBER 1944

▲ Panzer IV Ausf. J, 7th Company, II. Battalion, Panzer-Regiment 31, 5th Panzer-Division, Lithuania, Goldap sector, October 1944: final version of the Panzer IV, the Ausf. J was characterised by reinforced armour and reduced production costs, with the elimination of some non-essential components such as the commander's visor.

PANZER IV AUSF. J TANK, POLAND, MAY 1945

▲ Panzer IV Ausf. J, captured by the Poles, assigned to the 5th Armoured Artillery Squadron and later transferred to the 3rd Tank Training Regiment, Poland, May 1945: after its capture by Polish forces at the end of World War II, this Panzer IV Ausf. J was initially used for training purposes and later used as a vehicle for training new Polish armoured troops.

PANZER IV AUSF. J TANK, APRIL 1945

▲ Panzer IV Ausf. J, produced at the Nibelungenwerk, April 1945: this final version of the Panzer IV was manufactured in the last months of the Second World War. Production at the Nibelungenwerk continued until the end of the war, despite the bombing and gradual loss of territory.

BIBLIOGRAPHY

- Scheibert, Horst (1991). *The Panzer IV Family.* West Chester, PA: Schiffer Military History.
- Peter Chamberlain, Hilary Doyle e Thomas L. Jentz, *Encyclopedia of German Tanks of World War Two Revised edition*, Londra, Arms & Armour Press, 1993.
- AA.VV., *Panzer Aces Profiles - Guide to camouflage ans insignia.* Accion Press Madrid, Spain
- Bruce Culver, *PzKpfw IV in action*, Carrolton, Texas, Squadron/Signal Publications, inc., 1975,
- Walter J. Spielberger, Hilary L. Doyle, Thomas L. Jentz: *Panzer IV und seine Abarten.* Motorbuch Verlag, Stuttgart 2019
- Spielberger, Walter (1993). *Panzer IV and its variants.* Atglen, PA, USA: Schiffer Military History.
- AA.VV., *Pz.Kpfw. IV Ausf. F (Sd.Kfz. 161/1), in Panzer - I blindati tedeschi della seconda guerra mondiale*, n. 3, Novara, De Agostini, 2009
- Daniele Guglielmi, *Il Panzerkampfwagen IV,* in Storia Militare, n. 229, Parma, Ermanno Albertelli, ottobre 2012, pp. 28-36
- Wolfgang Fleischer: *Der Panzerkampfwagen IV – Rückgrat der deutschen Panzerverbände.* In: Waffen-Arsenal. Band 33. Podzun-Pallas, 2002,
- Doyle, Hilary; Jentz, Tom (2001). *Panzerkampfwagen IV Ausf. G, H and J 1942-45.* New Vanguard 39. Oxford, United Kingdom: Osprey.
- Jentz, Thomas; Doyle, Hilary (1997). *Panzer Tracts 4: Panzerkampfwagen IV - Grosstraktor to Panzerbefehlswagen IV.* Darlington Productions.
- Jentz, Thomas; Doyle, Hilary (2001). *Germany's Panzers in World War II: From Pz.Kpfw.I to Tiger II.* Atglen, PA: Schiffer Military History.
- Thomas Anderson: *Panzer IV.* Osprey Publishing, Oxford 2021
- Perrett, Bryan (1999). *Panzerkampfwagen IV Medium Tank : 1936-1945.* New Vanguard. Oxford, United Kingdom: Osprey.
- Vorschrift der Wehrmacht: *D 653/26 Panzerkampfwagen IV Fristenheft für Schmieren und Pflegearbeiten.* 1941
- Vorschrift der Wehrmacht: *D 653/25 Panzerkampfwagen IV (Sd.Kfz. 161) Ausführung A bis E - Pflegeheft.* 1939
- Caballero, Carlos; Molina, Lucas (October 2006). *Panzer IV: El puño de la Wehrmacht* (in Spanish). Valladolid, Spain: AFEditores.
- George Forty, *World War Two Tanks*, Osprey, 1995
- Robert Michulec, *Armor battles on the Eastern Front (1)*,Hong Kong, Concord pub.company,
- Dennis Oliver, *Panzer German army light tank*, Pen&Sword, Great Britain 2019.
- Fulvio Miglia, *Le armi del Terzo Reich, il Panzerkampfwagen III*, Roma, Bizzarri, 1974.
- Frido Maria von Senger und Etterlin, *Die deutschen Panzer 1926-1945*, Bernard & Graefe Verlag, 1973.
- Walter Spielberger Spielberger, Friedrich Wiener, *Die deutschen Panzerkampfwagen III und IV mit ihren Abarten*, Monaco, Lehmanns Verlag, 1968.
- Green, Michael; Anderson, Thomas; Schultz, Frank. *German Tanks of World War II.* London, UK: Zenith Imprints. ISBN 9781610607209.
- George Forty *Die deutsche Panzerwaffe im Zweiten Weltkrieg.* Bechtermünz, Augsburg 1998, ISBN 3-8289-5327-1.
- Ferdinand Maria von Senger und Etterlin *Die deutschen Panzer 1926–1945.* Bernard & Graefe, Bonn 1998, ISBN 3-7637-5988-3.

PUBLISHED TITLES

TWE-034 EN

www.ingramcontent.com/pod-product-compliance
Lightning Source LLC
LaVergne TN
LVHW070523070526
838199LV00072B/6692